Empathetic Echidna

Pippa Bird

In a peaceful corner of the Australian bush, there lived an echidna named Eddie.

Eddie was known far and wide for his kind heart and his special ability to understand and help his friends with their feelings.

One day, Eddie was wandering through the bush when he heard a soft sobbing sound. Following the sound, he found his friends, Bella and Bellamy Bilby sitting atop their burrow.

"Bella, what's troubling you?" Eddie asked.

Bella sighed, "I'm worried about the big storm that's coming. It'll be here on nightfall, I can smell it; I can feel the distant rumble in my feet."

They both looked toward the sky. It's blue hue was mixing
with pinks and yellows as the sun had begun to set.

"Oh yes, a storm is approaching," said Eddie.

"And the sun is soon to disappear. What if our burrow floods with the rain? It'll be dark…and I can't swim."

Just then, Penelope wanders over. "What is going on?
Why do you look so sad, my bilby friend?"

"Bella is afraid that the storm might wash into her burrow, and then she will have no home," said Eddie.

Penelope felt saddened for her friend. "You can come and live with me, Bella. I won't let my friend live without a home. Nobody should ever be without a home."

Bella sighed, but shook her head, "You live under water Penelope, it just wont work."

"Besides, I love my burrow. The sun shines through the trees perfectly, making it warm and cosy."

Bella started to cry, "…and it won't be after this storm if it's full of water."

"It's natural to feel worried," said Eddie, "Let's think of some ways to prepare and feel safer."

"We could gather rocks and sticks to reinforce your burrow," offered Penelope.

"Come on, let's go."

"Great idea, Penelope." Bella and Eddie chirped with excitement.

As the sun continued to disappear, dark clouds rolled in. Penelope, Eddie and Bella started collecting supplies to reinforce the burrow.

Esmeralda and Cookie overheard the conversation and
quickly started gathering supplies too.

All five of them spent dusk gathering sticks and
rocks to reinforce Bella's burrow.

As they raced against the approaching storm, Eddie talked to Bella about her feelings, helping her feel calmer and more in control.

By the time it had started to rain heavily, Bella felt much more secure.
She thanked her friends for being so generous with their help.

As water began to build up on the ground, Bella felt much better knowing she had done everything she could to keep her burrow dry until the rain passed.

Eddie continued to help his friends with their struggles, always listening and offering support.

His friends knew they could count on him to understand
their feelings and help them find ways to cope.

Eddie the Empathetic Echidna became a beloved figure in the bush, teaching everyone the importance of empathy and emotional support.

More from this series by Pippa Bird. Available on Amazon.

Calm Kangaroo — Mindfulness Alphabet

Quiet Quokka

Positive Platypus — Soula's Self-image

Co-regulating Koala — Lost and Found

Unwind with Calm Kangaroo

Positive Platypus — Posy's Special Find

Co-regulating Koala — Tumbling Tower

Co-regulating Koala — The Loud Crack

Wobbly Roo

Logical Lyrebird

Hop by Hop

Hop, Skip, Rest

Elated Emu

Corroborate Cockatoo

Kind Kookaburra

Timely Tarantula

Nonsense Numbat

Polite Python

Bully Bilby

About the Author
Pippa Bird is a former Mental Health Therapist in Private Practice Alula Blu Counselling Services, in regional NSW

Pippa holds a Bachelor in Psychology, a Diploma in Counselling, and a Diploma in Graphic Design, with a primary focus on illustration.

Calm Kangaroo

CALM KANGAROO is a backronym title for a children's mental and emotional well-being program. An initiative designed to educate children about mental health and foster a learning journey of emotional intelligence, resilience and cultivate an open mind through the benefits of reading well-being books, leading to the most important discussions and ideas.

CALM KANGAROO focuses on Curating, Advocating & Leading Mindfulness, & its mission to Kindle Awareness, Nurture Growth, Amplify Resilience, & Orchestrate Open-minds.

www.ingramcontent.com/pod-product-compliance
Lightning Source LLC
Chambersburg PA
CBHW060857270326
41934CB00003B/178

* 9 7 8 1 7 6 4 2 7 4 5 4 8 *